I Saw a

THIS
WAY

I saw a sign that said: WET FLOOR.

So I went out
the other door.

I saw a sign:
BEWARE OF GLASS!

4

KEEP OFF
THE GRASS

I saw a sign:

KEEP OFF THE GRASS.

I saw a sign.
This sign said: GO.

PLEASE
GO
SLOW

We had to drive on slowly, though.

I saw a sign:
ROADWORKS TODAY.

We went around
the other way.

I saw a sign
with words in red.
HARD HATS MUST BE
WORN, it said.

DANGER

HARD HATS
MUST BE WORN

Another sign said:
DUCKS CROSS HERE.

Just then I saw
the ducks appear.

Just when my day
seemed really great,
I saw a sign ...

WET
PAINT

a bit too late!